Cat Tales

Acknowledgments

*The author extends particular thanks to veterinarian Maud Lafon
for her invaluable help and to veterinary doctor Thierry Bédossa.*

Cat Tales

Claude Pacheteau

Photographs by Agence Horizon

Flammarion

Young male Persian, brown mackerel tabby

Contents

Sacred Cat of Burma, seal point

Preface

An Egyptian divinity, a creature alternately considered a portent of good fortune or of evil, a hunter of mice and other rodents, a symbol of the anarchist movement with its independent image, the sole companion of poets and writers, as well as the model of choice for painters and sculptors and an inspiration for composers, an oracle, a muse, a comic-strip hero, or advertising darling—few animals can pride themselves on being the source of so much passion, myth, or indeed superstition. An animal that, in the end, remains shrouded in mystery.

Puss, tomcat, pussycat: the list of names and nicknames likewise goes on, referring to the object of thousands of owners' adoration the world over and one who is very much part of the family.

Yet the cat is not without its disparagers when it comes to questions of overpopulation and the health risks it may incur.

This book is an invitation to meet with this lord of the urban and rural jungle—to discover its origins and evolution from the mists of time to the twenty-first century, tracing the path from its domestication by man to its status of cherished pet. It also seeks to portray the cat's checkered existence and relations with humankind, as well as provide information on the current distribution of the feline population and lifestyle. Finally, this book offers tips and advice on choosing a cat, and all that it entails, and on its education and care.

The second volume, dedicated to the various breeds, provides a detailed presentation of the most familiar to the most extraordinary.

Facing page: the cat, a mysterious (Sacred Cat of Burma, blue tabby)… and often independent being (right)

7

From past to present

Felidae appeared some forty-five million years ago. Several families successively came to light, including the paleofelidae and neofelidae whose morphology gradually altered in response to their needs for survival, their hunting manner, and habits. Findings of bones have made it possible to reconstruct this slow evolution leading to the cat as we know it today. Yet it is an evolution no less tinged with mystery.

Cats were apparently first domesticated in the seventh millennium B.C.E. At that time beauty did not enter the equation, and, at the very least, cats were not sought after for their grace or company, but rather for their ability to protect grain supplies from their sworn enemies—rats, mice, and other vermin.

The idea that the ancient Egyptians domesticated cats endured for a long time. The discovery of the remains of a cat alongside those of a human in a tomb in Cyprus came to refute this argument. Other researchers mention Persia or Libya as the cradle of the cat's domestication.

Yet the fact remains that the ancient Egyptians genuinely worshipped the cat. They even deified it as Bastet, the guardian goddess of the city of Bubastis. The large number of mummified sacred cats and their depictions on frescos further attest to this veneration.

Bastet, the cat-goddess
Bastet was the daughter of the sun god Ra. The ruins of

Facing page: female cat sarcophagus, Egypt, Eighth Dynasty, reign of Amenophis III (Egyptian Museum, Cairo)

Male Egyptian Mau, brown spotted tabby

the temple dedicated to her at Tell Basta (the House of Bastet), another name for Bubastis, can still be visited today. Some historians agree that of all the temples of the same period it would have been the finest.

Bastet's influence was not confined to Bubastis, and she was venerated throughout the land from the Sixth Dynasty (reign of Pepi II). Many votive objects dedicated to the goddess have been found at Saqqara. Not far from there, the funerary complex of Teti contained a large number of mummified cats.

Bastet was the guardian of women and children. Her powers enabled her to stimulate love and carnal energy. She was also the goddess of childbirth, a symbol of motherhood and womanhood, represented in the form of a cat-headed goddess or female cat. Yet her mildness was quite relative as she was also at times depicted with the head of a lioness, thereby identifying with another goddess—Sekhmet, the goddess of war. Both cat and lioness, gentle but cruel, she embodied woman as the guardian of the household. The Egyptians of the Late Period raised infants and kittens together, and texts report how some children would receive a few drops of blood from these kittens in order to protect them from disease.

Other legends surround the figure of Bastet, claiming her to be the wife of Atum, the mother of the lion god Mihos and the bearer of Pharaoh whom she suckled.

A turbulent history

Commercial exchanges led to the cat being discovered by the Greeks, probably around 500 B.C.E. Exported by the Egyptians, who had until then jealously guarded its secret, the cat was given the curious name of *ailouros* meaning "tail waver." In the second century B.C.E., it was *katoikidios* ("domestic"). Cats are found in Greek art, both in painting and pottery, even if the features remain fairly crude. In his *Description of Egypt*,

Egyptian mummified cats (Musée des Confluences, Lyons)
Following pages: two Norwegians. From left to right: male, red blotched tabby; and female, blue blotched tabby

Greece discovered cats c. 500 B.C.E.

Herodotus made first mention of the cat without going into further detail.

It was then the turn of the Roman Empire to succumb to the cat, which made its appearance among the wealthy classes before becoming more democratic. The Romans first called it *faeles* or *felis* (in the feminine), a term referring to wild carnivores. Though widely represented elsewhere, cats seldom appeared in Roman art, thus suggesting that it took them some time to become integrated into this civilization.

In the Middle Ages, cats spread to most parts of Europe, where they were similarly prized for their rat-catching prowess both by country folk and by monks in monasteries. Yet they would have to be patient before winning acclaim in the West and gaining the status of domestic animal in their own right. Though covered by legal writs, as in Wales, or with certain cats—such as those from the royal granaries—enjoying better protection than others, they still fell prey to man. During the harsh winters, they were coveted for their fur—including by the monks in monasteries. The symbol of too much independence—except for their hunting

Black cats have been the focus of many superstitions

prowess, cats contributed very little—they soon came to embody lewdness and to symbolize misfortune, being associated with the image of witches and other demons, as well as fueling all kinds of beliefs.

The first cat shows appeared in Great Britain in the late nineteenth century—in 1871 at London's Crystal Palace to be more specific. Siamese, Abyssinians, and Persians were exhibited there. In the United States, cats started to become widespread in the eighteenth century and the first feline beauty parade was organized in 1895, at Madison Square Garden in New York. Cats appear to have arrived in Canada with the Europeans. The first domestic cat to have set paw there was allegedly brought over by Father Le Caron in 1615.

Myths and superstitions

As much as cats were adulated in antiquity (notably in ancient Egypt), they then became the victims of beliefs making them out to be diabolical beings and the darling of witches. Crossing the path of a black cat was akin to walking under a ladder—and all the more disastrous if the cat was coming from the left! This persistent superstition still endures today.

The Middle Ages (chiefly from the fifth to the fifteenth century) had a dramatic impact on the feline population, which underwent true persecution. In Europe, the witchcraft trials conducted against practitioners of pagan rites led to the progressive disappearance of cats, verging on complete extinction. In the thirteenth century, the Inquisition portrayed the witch as a solitary creature accompanied by her cat. This is why many old women were tortured, burned alive, or drowned along with their cats.

Cats were considered the Devil's representative. They were even fitted with iron shoes so that they could be heard at night; one could thus avoid encountering them. If a funerary cortege crossed a cat's path, this was a presage of death for one of those present. Therefore, the mere sight of a small feline meant that the whole cortege would not hesitate to take a different route to reach the cemetery. In 1233, black cats were considered to be Satan incarnate, unless they happened to have a patch of white on the frontal bib. This marking, known as the "angel mark" or "God's finger," may have saved the cats' owners from a death sentence.

Another legend has it that witches have the ability to turn themselves into cats nine times in a row. This belief is not unrelated to that of a cat having nine lives. The Egyptians were already convinced that the cat could be reincarnated nine times given its ability to survive accidents such as falling from a great height. Why nine? This would appear to date back to ancient religious beliefs that the number nine had mystical properties.

On the use of cats

Even if the Church fostered the myth of the diabolical cat, not everyone was of the same opinion—notably country folk who prized the cat's ability to hunt down mice and other vermin. This helped to redress the balance in the cat's favor. In the early Middle Ages, cats were welcome guests of monks in monasteries, where they were highly instrumental in protecting grain supplies. With plague epidemics having decimated one third of Europe's human population, an ecclesiastical edict once again authorized the presence of cats in convents, from where they had been prohibited. In fact, this decision constituted the sole means of effectively eradicating the carriers of disease. In London in 1665, for example, the last epidemic of plague broke out when the decision to get rid of the cats had been passed.

Yet cats were not out of harm's way for all that, as rites and superstitions still lingered. The shameless slaughter of cats continued. Louis XIV, for example, finally outlawed the burning of cats in Paris on the Place

In England, white cats have always been considered a bad omen

15

The Laundry Woman; the cat is a figure in its own right in this scene painted by Chardin (Nationalmuseum, Stockholm)

The Nursing Mother; the cat is once again a symbol of motherhood (Marguerite Gérard, Musée Fragonard, Grasse)

de Grève during Midsummer's Day festivities, where it had become a "tradition."

The end of the witch-hunt in the late eighteenth century allowed cats to regain their status of domestic animal. Once again, as good hunters, they would keep watch over crops, supplies, and dwellings, and, in all likelihood thanks to them, there were no further outbreaks of the plague after 1790.

As in Europe, cats were appreciated across the Atlantic and across the Channel for their rat-catching prowess. Their talents were called on in the countryside to protect supplies and likewise during shipping. The navigator Jacques Cartier thus forbade any member of the crew to importune the cats that were taken on board during expeditions as a matter of course. Their role was to watch over supplies and to protect them from predators (such as rats and mice).

Though things have changed today, the role of protector is still topical. Several Los Angeles police departments and parking lots use feral cats in programs by the animal welfare group Voice for the Animals in order to repel vermin that attempt to infiltrate these establishments. As compensation for their good and loyal services, the cats are saved from euthanasia.

Symbol of good fortune and evil spells

Cats have long been both a symbol of good fortune and wealth and of misfortune and evil spells. The black cat—which immediately springs to mind—was not the sole target of superstitions that remained very deep-seated in rural areas in the early twentieth century. Crossing the path of a cat, whatever its color, was never a good sign, particularly if the encounter took place on the first day of the year. Some would have no qualms about postponing an appointment if they came across a

Facing page: cat of the Russian Blue breed

Puss in Boots (a fairy tale by Perrault); illustration from a Poulain chocolate bar (1954)

cat on the way. A cat looking to be stroked was an omen of future betrayal; a cat presented as a gift was considered in the same way as knives and other sharp objects—a potential breaker of friendship.

On the other hand, a cat sneezing beside a bride-to-be was the portent of a happy marriage. In England, cats were perceived rather as bearers of good luck—and still are to this day—black cats included. Yet, white cats were a bad sign. In Brittany, a region rich in legends, medicinal virtues were attributed to white cats. Drops of blood from the ear of a white female were believed to cure pneumonia. In Sweden and Finland, cats were considered to be imps with the power to bring riches to humankind, while in Germany they were capable of stocking up the larder! In the Far East, cats are seen as lucky animals. Chinese merchants would keep a cat tied up in their store; if it ran away, their prosperity would suffer.

In the United States, white cats can be both unlucky (if encountered at night) and lucky (if appearing in a dream).

In the eighteenth and nineteenth centuries, the English insisted on having at least one black cat on their ships. Later, the insurance company Lloyds refused to insure sailing vessels that did not carry a certain number of cats on board, at least one of which had to be black! Legend also has it that Napoleon crossed the path of a black cat shortly before doing battle in Waterloo, thus imparting good luck to the English.

And finally, the cat's image of independence has always been so strong that in the nineteenth century it became the symbol of the anarchist movement.

A creature of culture

Cats have inspired many writers and novelists. Some, like the writer Ernest Hemingway, vowed true passion to them. His house on the small island of Key West in Florida had no less than some fifty cats.

Some authors have made the cats in their works into strange protagonists, coming from who-knows-where. They include Howard Phillips Lovecraft or David Weber whose cat became an extraterrestrial. Edgar Allan Poe, considered a master by Lovecraft, possessed a vision of the animal verging on the ghostly (*The Black Cat and Other Stories*).

Cat and dog join forces to help themselves to provisions in this kitchen where the maidservant is distracted from her work by the master of the house (Beaussant & Lefèvre)

Frequently appearing in works of science fiction, cats are often schemers (*The Voyage of the Space Beagle* by Alfred Elton Van Vogt) or victims as in *The Invisible Man* by H.G. Wells.

Authors continue to feature cats in novels today. Examples include Carol Nelson Douglas and her hero Midnight Louie, or the writer Rob Reger (*Emily the Strange: I Wanna be your Cat*).

Cats have also been one of the main characters in fairy tales for children, even if they make a more or less furtive appearance as in Lewis Carroll's *Alice's Adventures in Wonderland* and *Through the Looking-Glass* in which Alice's little cat was also found on the other side of the looking-glass.

The writer Samuel Johnson (1709–84) is a well-known figure among English cat lovers. The statue of his companion, named Hodge, sits enthroned in front of its master's former residence. It was unveiled in 1997 at 17 Gough Square, London.

The British are also quite familiar with Humphrey, the most popular English cat, who was the last feline resident at 10 Downing Street. This black and white, longhaired cat spent eight years as Chief Mouser there. A little runaway, it once turned up at the Royal Army Medical College and was almost run over by Bill Clinton's Cadillac on one of his visits. Allergic to cats, Cherie Blair, the wife of Tony Blair, demanded Humphrey's departure when the couple moved into Downing Street. Humphrey then lived with a Cabinet Office worker until the cat's death in 2006.

The United States also boasts feline celebrities like Oscar. This cat, said to have the ability to predict impending death, is "used" in an American hospice and has made it into the US press. Cinnamon is another example. This four-year-old Abyssinian cat lives at the American University of Missouri-Columbia and belongs to Dr. Kristina Narfstrom. Its distinguishing feature: to be the first cat whose genome was mapped. In 2007, 20,285 genes were identified, making Cinnamon one of America's stars.

The Americans were also the first to clone a cat. The achievement was made by researchers at the Faculty of Veterinary Medicine of Texas A&M University. Named Cc—Carbon Copy—this cat was born from the transplantation of eighty-two embryos in seven surrogate females in an operation costing more than $3.5 million.

On a final note, English and American trade literature may be deceptive for those lacking a full grasp of the language. For example, in some monographs on cat breeds, the "British (Shorthair)" is known as the "European Shorthair". This is enough to cause a fair

Male Highland Fold, blue and white

The cat's independence symbolized the anarchist movement in the nineteenth century

amount of confusion, as in other countries they are two quite distinct breeds.

Feline movie stars

The Cat from Outer Space, That Darn Cat!, The Incredible Journey—Disney studios have often staged cats in feature-length productions and cartoons. In the United States, Orangey is undoubtedly the feline actor best known to cinemagoers. This red tabby cat has around a dozen movies to his name, including Blake Edwards' *Breakfast at Tiffany's*, after a novel by Truman Capote, with Audrey Hepburn at his side. This role also earned him a Patsy Award, the animal world's equivalent of an Oscar. Subsequently renamed Minerva by his mistress, he was also nicknamed the feline Clark Gable in the United States and the feline Laurence Olivier in Great Britain.

On a musical note

In 1991, Freddie Mercury, lead singer of the rock band Queen, released *Innuendo*. It included a track entitled *Delilah*, dedicated to his cat of the same name. In 1985, Freddie Mercury had already dedicated his first solo album, *Mr. Bad Guy*, to "cat lovers everywhere."

Proverbs and expressions

"It's raining cats and dogs" is a strange saying of unknown origin that indicates heavy rain. In England, many proverbs mention cats, including "care will kill a cat," "while the cat's away, the mice will play," and "a cat may look at a king." Some of these expressions or proverbs are also found in other countries.

The equivalent of some foreign proverbs have lost their reference to cats in English. They are idioms: "Two can play that game" (*A bon chat, bon rat* in French, literally "For every good cat, a good rat"); "Once bitten, twice shy" (*Chat échaudé craint l'eau froide* in French, literally "Scalded cat fears cold water"); "I have a frog in my throat" (whereas the French have a cat, *J'ai un chat dans la gorge*); "To have other fish to fry," which has an equivalent expression "to have other cats to flag" in some countries. Where some nations might "set the wolf among the sheepfold," the English "set the cat among the pigeons." And "to let the cat out of the bag" becomes "to sell the wick" elsewhere.

Writers, politicians, and other celebrities have also coined "feline" quotations:

- One of the most striking differences between a cat and a lie is that a cat has only nine lives. *Mark Twain*

- A cat has absolute emotional honesty: human beings, for one reason or another, may hide their feelings, but a cat does not. *Ernest Hemingway*

- A lark's leg is better than a whole roast cat. *John Heywood*

- Dogs look up to us. Cats look down on us. Pigs treat us as equals. *Winston Churchill*

Cat and mouse: an inexhaustible source of inspiration

How do cats work?

All over the world, the cat has now become a member of the family in its own right in the same way as the dog. They are pampered—sometimes even to excess—which can lead to anthropomorphic attitudes in their masters. A cat is a cat. Like a dog, it should know its place and respect the rules of the household.

Even if a cat is not trained in the same way as a dog, there are certain basic guidelines that should be respected by all of the family so that the cat can have its rightful place in the household and the relationship, set to last for many years—it is not rare for a cat to celebrate its twentieth birthday—is harmonious.

More relational problems have emerged over the past few years between owners and their cats. Consulting a behaviorist is not only the preserve of dog-owners. Urine markings, damage, rebellion—cats are not exempt from such faults, which are not limited to dogs. Soiling in cats may have several causes including insufficient cleaning of its litter tray, the presence of a new cat in the house, moving house, or a change in its environment.

The solution? Take the education or re-education of one's cat in hand without delay. This can take the form of simple things and attitudes: the master needs to assert himself as the leader of the pack. He is the decision maker; it is he who chooses when it is time for meals, cuddles, or games.

Sixty million cats were recorded in a European census.

Cats are thought of as being highly independent creatures, yet they are nothing of the sort. Variations in character do of course exist, depending on the breed of cat. A Chartreux or a Persian is reputedly more adaptable than a Siamese for instance. But that is not everything. Education and the way you behave with your companion will be the deciding factors in the relationship you develop.

The earlier you accustom your kitten to being handled, brushed, or washed, the easier it will be as it gets older. The use of games for educative purposes and tasty treats as rewards (within reason!) will be invaluable allies.

In 2002, the Association of Pet Behavior Counsellors took charge of more than 714 cats in order to solve behavioral problems. This is quite significant. In 29 percent, the problems encountered were behavior-related—mainly house soiling (29 percent), urine marking or claw marks (22 percent), or certain forms of aggressiveness toward humans (12 percent). In detail, out of the 1,853 cats who participated in this survey, 1,389 demonstrated a behavioral problem: 325 concerning cleanliness, 158 excessive grooming, 103 aggressiveness, 201 aggressiveness toward the other cats in the house, 107 hyper-attachment with separation anxiety, 75 destructiveness (claw marks), and 34 for "abnormal" sexual behavior.

According to this survey, males appear 1.5 times as "talkative" as females, 1.5 times as aggressive toward unfamiliar cats, exhibit three times the number of problems

related to cleanliness, and seven times more inappropriate sexual behavior. Females, for their part, were shown to be 1.5 times more excessively irritable than males. These issues denote a real behavioral problem, which is often due to the master who may be unaware of this. Do not hesitate to contact the breeder or veterinarian to settle any problems that arise, or better still, think ahead to avoid them.

In addition to behaviorists (veterinarians or other), there are associations that aim to help owners to foster a healthy relationship with their cat. In the United Kingdom, for example, this takes the form of the FAB (Feline Advisory Bureau), a charitable organization that

---

Facts and figures

In the USA:
- 31.6 percent of households have at least one cat.
- Average number of cats per household: 2.1.
- US$178.50: the average amount spent each year on veterinary treatment.
- Almost two-thirds of pet-owners in the United States allow their dog or cat to sleep in their bed, and buy them gifts at Christmas.

In Great Britain:
- For the sake of their cat, 48 percent of owners questioned in a survey would be prepared to move house, 60 percent would postpone vacation, and 48 percent would get into debt.
- For 82 percent, their cat helps them overcome stress and to relax.
- For 62 percent, it reduces lonesomeness; 75 percent prefer to share their feelings with their cat than with human beings.
- Owners spent 708 million pounds on cat food in 2006.

Only 3 percent of owned cats belong to a cat breed

seeks to promote progress in the areas of feline health and wellness among cat owners and breeders. The FAB organizes and subsidizes conferences for veterinary colleges and symposiums. Experts participate and share their knowledge with other veterinary practitioners, breeders, and cat owners.

Think of cats and you think of "purring." Yet cats do not always purr in contentment. As soon as kittens suckle on their mother, they utter this sound that is synonymous with pleasure. The cat will keep this form of expression through to adulthood. Yet some cats never purr. Don't forget either that cats also purr in stressful situations—at the veterinarian or when sick, injured, and in pain. In fact, it is their way of saying that they need looking after.

While dogs and cats were not originally designed for cohabitation—and even less so for getting along together—it is man who led these two species to live together, sometimes in quite close quarters. The fact that they do not share the same codes of communication does not facilitate their mutual understanding of emotions and intentions—postures, gesticulations, or sounds uttered may have different meanings. And it is possible to observe that some of their signals—nonetheless virtually identical—in fact express states and, by extension, messages that are at times completely opposed. They may give rise to misunderstandings, which does not make for harmonious relations!

With nothing more than a wave of their tails, cats and dogs do indeed express quite opposite emotions. When a dog wags its tail from left to right, this is a sign of clear friendliness toward another dog, a desire to play, or of a state of well being; when a cat does the same thing, it means annoyance and even open hostility. Yet

With almost seventy million cats present in American homes, the cat is the most popular pet in the United States

rituals. After a period of more or less extended foreplay, the sexual act itself is swift. In the presence of a female in heat, the male tends to make significantly more markings, urine in particular.

Females generally enter puberty at the age of around nine to ten months. This is influenced by the seasons (the first estrus usually arrives during the course of the first spring after the cat's birth) and the environment (presence of other cats, adult males, that favor the onset of puberty, although overpopulation may conversely delay it). Sexual activity also depends on breed. Orientals are reputed for having an earlier puberty, while this occurs later in Persians in particular.

Males reach puberty at the age of around eight to ten months. In some breeds (such as Persians and their derivatives) physiological puberty does not concur with behavioral puberty, which means that a male may be fertile but too immature to accomplish the act of mating. On a final note, males exhibit continuous sexual behavior throughout their lives and can therefore mate with a female in estrus regardless of the time of year.

Male Exotic Shorthair kitten, brown spotted tabby

if cat and dog are accustomed to living together at a very early age, their cohabitation is quite possible.

Olfaction plays a very important role in the way cats communicate on a daily basis. Through pheromones given off by their bodies or set down in selected places, cats leave signals (urine markings, claw marks, facial marks by rubbing against objects or living beings) that correspond to various situations—perhaps to assert their belonging to a group, place, or to convey their emotional state or to define their spatial location. This means of communication is also used during mating

Facing page: a European law now exists to protect cats
Following pages: the low vaccination rate for cats represents
a high health risk in Europe

Pedigree cats: some guidelines

Given the fact that several cat associations exist in the United Kingdom, the United States and Canada, classifications, breed standards, and the number of breeds officially recognized may vary. The differences mainly concern the cat's physical characteristics rather than behavior, which does not change from one country to another. These physical criteria, compiled and set out in the breed standards, form the benchmark for judging in cat shows, which are organized by one of the official cat federations.

Some associations consider certain breeds of cat as a variety belonging to another breed, while for others they form a breed in their own right. This is the case with, for example, the Javanese, Colorpoint, Shorthair, Bombay, or Himalayan. Furthermore, some associations fail to recognize certain breeds. Neither the Fédération Internationale Féline (FIFe) nor the Governing Council of the Cat Fancy (GCCF) recognize the Scottish Fold; the Ragdoll is not recognized by the Cat Fanciers Association (CFA) but is by The International Cat Association (TICA) and the FIFe; and the Bengal is recognized only by TICA.

In the case of polydactyl cats, for instance, they may be registered for shows in America. Accepted by the CFA, TICA, the American Cat Fanciers

Association (ACFA), and the Cat Fanciers Federation (CFF), these cats—whose distinctive feature lies in their number of toes—are not eligible for similar "favors" elsewhere.

It can be hard for a novice to make sense of all this at times. Yet these federations all share a common mission—namely to keep track of all the breeds of cats they recognize by maintaining a book of origins. They are also responsible for issuing pedigrees for purebred cats born on their soil and under their jurisdiction, managing the various standards and their

Each breed has its own standard
Facing page: a black and white, female Cornish Rex
Various books of origins exist that provide breed inventories
Right: a female Chartreux

modifications (such as recognizing new colors, for example), training judges, monitoring cat shows, and validating titles for their ratification. One of the other main tasks of these federations is their mission to promote pedigree cats in order to bring them to the public's attention and to assist would-be cat owners. The notion of pedigree cats is not always very clear to the public at large, which is apt to turn to the pet-shop network, which offers much less surety in terms of health or behavior as compared with enthusiastic fanciers and professional breeders.

Breeders also enjoy a privileged relationship with these structures in areas such as animal counseling or breeding conduct. They address their requests for cat pedigrees to them. The GCCF issues an estimated thirty thousand pedigrees each year. Without this key, a cat cannot be labeled "pedigree" or "purebred." Even if it seems to fit the bill, it will be termed "-type" and will

---

Favorite breeds

In the United States (where cats outnumber dogs 75 million to 60 million), the public's top ten favorite breeds are the Persian, the Maine Coon, the Exotic, the Abyssinian, the Siamese, the Ragdoll, the Sphynx, the Birman, the American Shorthair and the Oriental.

In England, cats also prevail over dogs (over 9.6 million individuals to 6.8 million canine companions) and the preference goes to the British Shorthair in first place, which has succeeded in ousting the Persian. The latter takes second position, followed by the Siamese.

In Canada, there are some 4.8 million cats and the three most popular breeds are the Persian, the Himalayan, and the Siamese.

The Persian is a highly popular breed

Sacred Cat of Burma

be unable to aspire to shining on the podiums of cat beauty parades.

It is therefore thanks to the work of breeders, who are above all selectors, that breeds of cat are able to endure throughout the world, with variants inherent in each country's official texts that serve as reference. Selective breeders preserve the morphological and behavioral characteristics of the cats they produce.

In addition to respecting the standard, they also do the groundwork for socialization, which the owner should continue after purchasing his kitten. These professionals and enthusiastic amateurs are therefore the guarantors of the continuity of breeds of cat and ensure that the descendants of their stud or queen comprise kittens healthy in both mind and body. Few countries are spared from problems linked to the trade in wildlife. All cat associations therefore stress the argument of traceability.

European Shorthair kitten, brown spotted tabby

What's in a standard?

More than a classification of cats according to their hair type and morphology, it is the standard that acts as reference. This text is the detailed description of the ideal, perfect cat, although it is well known that no subject fits the bill 100 percent. Yet some get quite close, and this is what sets them apart from others in cat shows. A breed standard also lists the faults that lead to penalties or disqualification during the judging of beauty contests.

The standard provides the breed's genotype, as well as the outcrossing possibilities (mating with other breeds) as there is no question of breeders playing Dr. Frankenstein.

A scale of points is also established, varying from one breed to another, which makes it possible to grade coat and color, hair texture, or shape of body or head. Each cat association throughout the world has its own scale of points.

On a final note, a breed standard can be modified over time depending on how the breed in question evolves, in order to respond to breeders' efforts at selection. Even if would-be purchasers are not looking for a cat to do the rounds of the shows, by taking the trouble to consult the standard they will be able to refine their choice and thereby avoid certain errors.

A wide range of prices

The price of a pedigree cat depends on what you are looking for exactly—a future champion show cat (some cats are known to command thousands of dollars), an exceptional queen or stud, or a pet. The fact nonetheless remains that, for a pedigree cat, being a good companion and quite worthy of its standard are not incompatible notions. Only the price will be lower if you are simply looking for a good pet. Other things to consider are the questions of rarity, which may influence the price, and certain medical aspects. Strange as it may seem, some vaccinations are not obligatory when selling cats. Serious breeders who have their kittens inoculated therefore incur supplementary costs. Some also call for examinations as a means of ensuring the absence of any genetic defect in the parents. All this comes at a price and in the end is a question of quality—the assurance of having a healthy cat of good lineage, whose behavioral tendencies are basically predetermined.

There is a scale of points for each breed, in order to note various characteristics. Facing page: an Abyssinian

The best known and the most rare

Not all breeds come under the same heading. While the Persian is undoubtedly the world's best-known cat, there are some breeds that can be classified as being very rare. For example, in France, a dozen breeds exist for which no birth has been registered for four years. They include the Bombay Japanese, the Californian Rex, the Cymric, or the Don Sphynx.

There are countless reasons for this, such as lack of public or breeder interest, or difficulty of selection and production.

Would-be cat owners therefore have some sixty breeds to choose from in all. To simplify the task, and to classify them according to the physical criteria that clearly differentiate them, cat breeds are generally divided into two categories of hair length: short and

Today, cats are grouped into two categories: short hair and long hair. Above: a female Siamese, cinnamon point

long, with Persians and their majestic coats belonging to the latter category. These categories of hair type are then divided into different morphological groups. Body types include the "rangy" (or "oriental"), and the generally athletic cats in this group have slender figures. Among the worthy representatives of this group is the Siamese, certainly one of the most well known, or the Oriental. As well as their physical characteristics, these cats have a reputation for being active and therefore requiring a master with time to devote to them.

Then there are "medium conformation" cats (cobby, semi-foreign, or foreign), notable examples of which are the Abyssinian or the Sphynx. This is a varied category but is mainly composed of cats that, while active in their behavior, know how to remain discreet.

"Compact" (or cobby) cats include the Persian, the Burmese, or even the Chartreux.

Some breeds of cat can be classified as giants. This is the case of the Maine Coon or the Norwegian to name but two, whose size sometimes exceeds that of a small breed of dog!

The head, muzzle, coat, ears and eyes of each breed are also carefully defined. The head may be broad or full-cheeked, round, square, a wedge, or blunt, with prominent cheekbones; the muzzle may have prominent whisker pads or whisker pinches and a strong jaw or chin; the ears may be large or small, with rounded tips, erect, alert, or slightly pointed; the coat may be fine, glossy or silky, smooth or lustrous, or dense, plush, and full of life; eyes may be large, round, and full, with an oriental slant, or bright, clear and alert.

Breeders are not born in a day

Cat breeding is a regulated trade (registered as a business, declared with the board of veterinary services, and

Some breeds are very rare, like this female Sphynx, tortie mackerel tabby and white

in possession of a certificate of eligibility). On the one hand, there are professionals for whom this is their main activity, and on the other, "enthusiastic amateurs" for whom it is not the sole activity. Yet both are worlds apart from those cat dealers or private individuals who are motivated simply by the lure of gain. A breeder or serious amateur earns very little money from breeding—and sometimes marks more loss than profit! A litter entails much expense in such areas as food, care, vaccinations, and identification.

Breeding also requires a large investment in terms of time and availability. Breeders need to know all there is to know about the breed they are raising, ensure the births, monitor the young, be on hand for would-be cat owners looking for a kitten, and attend shows to promote their cattery.

This line of business, which can be guided only by passion and the love of a breed, is not for everyone.

Overbreeding in the hot seat

Breeds of cat, like their canine counterparts, have developed over time. It is through the efforts of selective breeders that subjects are produced in keeping with the standard. However, there is sometimes a tendency towards "overbreeding", or inbreeding. Inbreeding refers to breeding two cats together that are very closely related, in order to favot the development of certain physical characteristics. This is often to satisfy the demands of a particular clientele ever on the lookout for "bigger" or "more extraordinary" cats. Breeders worth their salt indeed avoid overbreeding as it is known to be a source of potential health issues,

Siesta in the sun—the favorite
pastime of certain cats

Felis silvestris lybica attacking a cobra

The cat will have the last word!

such as respiratory or sinus problems in flat-faced breeds for example, or eye and dental problems. In many countries, breeders are concerned that one day certain breeds will be prohibited because of the genetic health risks associated with the breed. This subject has been touched upon in both dogs and cats whose morphology some see as a source of discomfort for the animal's health and wellbeing.

Wildcats and alley cats

Novices tend to confuse European and alley cats. The European is indeed a breed in its own right, which is not the case for the alley cat. Alley cats form the most widespread breed in France (more than 95 percent of the feline population); they are so well known and popular that the official authorities have decided to admit them to the sacrosanct cat beauty shows. They are judged in the "house-cat" category. A "Ratter's Club" was even formed in the early 1930s in Normandy, France, but was short-lived. The European's popularity has a flipside—being widespread and well liked, it is the cat on which least attention (identification, medical care) is lavished, given its lack of market value. The image of the cat as a free spirit, which quite spontaneously springs to mind, also explains this lack of interest.

There are other varieties of "wild" cats, generally brown in color with black stripes and whose height does not exceed 31.5 inches (80 centimeters) and weight 13 pounds (6 kilograms). They live mainly in Africa, Western Asia, and Europe. These cats belong to three sub-species: *Felis silvestris lybica*, *Felis silvestris catus*, and *Felis silvestris silvestris*. They have the distinctive feature of being able to adapt to their environment and although protected, they are a target for hunters. In Africa, the desert and the savannah are their chosen territory, and certain theories argue that

Felis silvestris silvestris, a variety of "wildcat"

these wildcats could be the ancestors of the domestic cat, particularly with the discovery of feline remains alongside those of a human in a tomb in Cyprus dating from the seventh millennium B.C.E.

Choosing your kitten

Adopting a cat—whether an alley or pedigree—is no lightweight matter! Far from trifling, this decision will commit the would-be owner for over ten or sometimes twenty years. In other words, it entails a heavy responsibility. The decision should therefore be deeply considered and have obtained the go-ahead from all the members of the household.

It should not be forgotten that adopting a cat—even an alley cat given away free of charge by an acquaintance—implies a certain budget for its food, maintenance, and health. In the main, the financial consequences of owning a cat are less than those of a dog, yet they are not insignificant and should be taken into account.

Once your mind is made up, patience is still the order of the day. Being well informed and visiting catteries, if considering the adoption of a pedigree cat, are indispensable groundwork and form part of the adoption procedure.

The abundance of information available in magazines and books about cats provides a good solution for an initial overview. The specialist feline press, works on cats, and Web sites are all sources of information, which also provide addresses of breeders. Word-of-mouth may likewise prove useful, particularly if there are cat lovers in your entourage.

Facing page: choosing a cat such as this male Maine Coon, harlequin brown blotched tabby and white, requires careful reflection

Each alley cat is unique

Pedigree or alley cat?

Pedigree cats make up a marginal population in the feline landscape, which is largely dominated by alley cats. The choice of a pedigree or alley cat is a matter of personal reflection, perhaps influenced by financial considerations.

The pedigree cat has a quite distinctive physical appearance, which is the result of long-term selection efforts and would be hard to find in an alley cat. If you are attracted by a physical characteristic typical of a breed—such as the Persian's squashed face or the

Professional breeders or enthusiastic fanciers are the best advisors when thinking of acquiring a cat
Above: English Burmese kittens, lilac and lilac tortie

Scottish Fold's curled ears—then the choice is easily made. If you are more undecided, visiting catteries and cat shows may help you make up your mind. And if physical appearance is of little concern, an alley cat will make an excellent companion, with the bonus feature of being unique!

Acquiring a pedigree cat implies a certain budget, in terms of the purchase price that can be fairly high, but which is justified by the cost of breeding and selection. To offset this, breeding provides a certain number of guarantees not only relating to the cat's future physique, but also to its character, which has been the subject of selections.

Selection criteria for pedigree cats

Once the decision has been made to purchase a pedigree cat, it remains to find your dream kitten. The choice of breed is governed by various criteria—color, hair length requiring varying degrees of maintenance, and price. Making inquiries at breed clubs and with breeders is an essential preliminary step before taking the leap.

Each kitten is different, even within the same litter. The breeder will be able to advise you by providing information on each kitten's character and suggesting which might suit you best. You might find love at first sight, which is difficult to ignore. Yet beware of letting yourself yield to the sickliest or least lively kitten, which is potentially the most fragile and therefore the most problematic.

A minimal check is required to ensure the kitten's good health—a glossy coat, alert attitude, eyes that are not watery, and the absence of earwax are all signs of a good general condition.

Commonly, the legal age set for sale is eight weeks. Yet the age of three months appears more appropriate to ensure that the kitten is fully socialized and so allow a good start in life.

Purebred kitten or alley cat? A matter of choice

Where to look

Acquaintances, classified ads in specialist publications, registers of litters compiled by breed clubs, cat shows where kittens are occasionally for sale, pet stores, and animal shelters are all possible channels for finding a cat.

Breeders remain the best guarantors of the quality and good health of your future kitten. In addition, they carry out an in-depth program of socialization and are able to provide information on the character of each kitten, thereby steering you toward the choice that is best for you.

Generally speaking, the reproduction period is at its peak in the spring. Kittens will therefore be at their most plentiful in this season and in summer.

The legal age for the sale of kittens in many countries is a minimum of eight weeks. Above: a Scottish Fold kitten

all, you will need to devote time to it, look after it, and play with it. In short, you should show concern for its happiness!

An adoption that has been well-prepared and carried out in due form is the first stage in a long journey alongside a unique companion, who will soon become absolutely irreplaceable.

Adult or kitten?

Usually we go for kittens, as a young age makes it easier for the cat to adapt to its new environment and allows a relation of complicity to be built up more swiftly. It is also enjoyable to watch as your companion grows up and to have your heart melt before the inimitable antics of kittens. Nonetheless, it is possible to consider adopting an adult cat from an animal shelter or from someone who is no longer able to keep it, thus combining pleasure and a good deed. More autonomous, already house-trained, and less boisterous, an adult cat is also less complicated to handle initially. To facilitate its adaptation, various tricks such as the use of soothing pheromones, on the advice of your veterinarian, may prove useful.

In order to authenticate the purchase, the breeder should deliver a certain number of documents: a passport, tattoo card or electronic ID certificate, certificate of transfer, pedigree, or a photocopy of the pedigree of the parents.

A long-term commitment

Whatever the course taken, the breed, the age, and the price paid if any, adopting a cat entails a long-term commitment. Whether purchased or given away, the cat or kitten will require care, attention, suitable quality food, as well as regular visits to the veterinarian. Above

Facing page: animal shelters offer
a large number of cats for adoption
Following pages: acquiring a cat entails
a commitment lasting, on average, some fifteen years

Getting ready to welcome a young cat

Aged ideally between eight and twelve weeks, the kitten arrives at its new home. This change of residence, a novel experience in its tender new existence, is no trivial matter for the kitten; your complying with a few guidelines will help to smooth the transition. If the little feline's arrival is handled badly, this is likely to leave a deep impression and negatively influence its later behavior.

The basic rule to respect is that the place of adoption should be in keeping with the place where it was bred. A kitten raised on a farm, isolated from other dwellings, will find it hard to adapt to city life. And vice versa—a kitten raised in town, who was handled regularly and well socialized, will suffer if it finds itself isolated in a dwelling in the middle of the countryside, alone all day long.

If this basic principle is respected, minimal preparation should be required to welcome a young animal.

A smooth arrival

A suitable secure cage should be used when transporting the kitten from the breeding site to its new home. Such traveling boxes are readily available in the stores. On arrival, you should reassure the kitten, who will of course have found the trip stressful and who must also discover an unknown place, full of unfamiliar

Young female Maine Coon, brown blotched tabby and white

smells—not forgetting that it has just been separated from its mother and siblings. It's quite a big deal for a little creature only two months old!

It is therefore advisable at first to place the kitten in just one room of the house, preferably a calm place where it will not be disturbed. Beforehand, you will

Facing page: the arrival of a kitten in its new home should be handled calmly

have set up a litter tray, a bowl of its usual food, and one of water.

Although the rest of the family will be clamoring to see the new arrival, they will have to be patient and let the kitten get used to its environment before coming to say hi. Too much emotion too soon and too many new faces at once are likely to be stressful for the kitten.

The initial contact with the house's occupants should be smooth, in a reassuring setting, generated by caresses and soft words. There is no point in throwing yourself on the kitten and petting it all over! Let it come to you and get to know you at its own pace.

After a few days of isolation and repeated contacts with the family members, it is time for the new arrival to explore its new home. To do so, you should let it gain access progressively to the other rooms so that it can discover and become accustomed to this new living environment, which will become its territory.

Games and accessories

For the kitten's well-being, it is essential to provide some games. You don't need to invest in expensive toys—a simple cork attached to a piece of string will do quite nicely. It is important for the kitten to be able to amuse itself and to while away its solitude when left alone.

Play is vital for the cat's development—even when very young, it played with its brothers and sisters. Once away from its siblings, it needs to be able to play alone or with its new owners.

Cats have retained a highly developed hunting instinct, which is demonstrated in predatory behavior aimed at objects or other living beings (such as rodents and birds). This activity is crucial to their natural

Kittens, like this young male Snowshoe, are incessantly playful and are attracted by everything around them

balance, and they have to find a way of exerting it in their living space, all the more so if they cannot go outside. There is no need to complicate things here, as a simple ball can suffice.

In any event, don't skip the games and toys. As well as providing entertainment for the kitten, they allow it to enhance its curiosity and are essential to its development.

More sophisticated devices, including cat trees, scratching posts, and catnip, can put the finishing touches to your kitten's small world. Scratching posts also allow it to trim its claws, which is very useful if living in an apartment. Cat trees are versatile, as they generally include a scratch pad, but also provide a play area and place to rest. Though more expensive to buy, they are also more comprehensive and particularly useful if space is limited.

First trip to the veterinarian

Once the kitten has settled into its new home, there is someone else it must meet—the veterinarian. In theory, on arrival the kitten should already have had its first vaccinations and been identified and wormed. The new owner should now take over, carrying out basic care and attending to vaccinations and worming.

Ideally, you should make an appointment with a practitioner who will update vaccinations, prescribe a suitable worming treatment, and explain how to administer it. In theory, cats should be wormed every month until the age of six months; thereafter, depending on the situation and the living environment, two to four times a year, even more in a breeding center or if the cat is exhibited in shows. Vaccination is subject to annual boosters.

The first trip to the veterinarian is an opportunity for the practitioner to do a full medical checkup and to verify that the kitten is healthy. He will also prescribe an

The cat is an animal with a strong instinct for hunting

Kittens will quickly explore a home's smallest nooks and crannies

"Curious as a cat," as the saying goes!

external parasiticide to deal with fleas and ticks. The kitten must be treated, even if living in an apartment, as fleas are unwanted guests that develop easily in dwellings, brought in by outside channels (such as visitors and animals).

The veterinarian will also advise on various products specifically designed for cat hygiene, such as shampoos or eye and ear cleansers.

Kits for cats

Adopting a cat means having to invest in a minimum of equipment for the comfort and cleanliness of its body and soul. A litter tray is indispensable; it can range from a simple plastic tray to a sophisticated box with cover and reserve tank. The choice depends on your taste and pocket. Be sure to choose one whose sides are high enough to stop the contents from spilling over onto the floor. Once you have the tray, it remains to buy the litter. Various kinds of litter are available on the market, sometimes with a deodorant incorporated. Yet this is no excuse for failing to clean the tray regularly; highly sensitive to odor and cleanliness, the cat will not want to use it if dirty. Ideally, the tray should be set in a quiet place, away from the source of food and the sleeping area, as the cat makes a distinction between these places.

Besides the litter, two bowls are required: one for water and the other for food.

The range of sleepware—baskets, hampers, and cushions—available in the stores is also very wide. The important thing is that the cat has a place of its own where it can rest peacefully without being disturbed.

All kittens are adorable, like this fine litter of Scottish Folds

Educating a young cat

Cats are fascinating creatures and their "handling" should respect their characteristic features. It is therefore pointless to think of educating a cat in the same way as a dog because such an undertaking would be destined for failure from the outset.

Territorial animals with the deserved reputation of being hunters, cats are paradoxically able to live very happily in an apartment. Despite their solid reputation of independence, cats do indeed enjoy their masters' company and suffer if they must be left alone all day.

However, unlike dogs—pack animals that need a dominant chief and will do anything to please him—cats do not learn in order to please their master but for their own pleasure!

Moreover, unlike dogs, cats have not undergone a utilitarian selection (for hunting, guard, or rounding up flocks) and are therefore not conditioned to fulfill a role. The set of orders that might be taught is consequently more limited.

Cats should therefore not be left to their own devices but should be given a minimum amount of education, which is useful as a foundation for serene cohabitation in the household.

Facing page: play is an excellent means of educating a cat; here, a female Siberian, Neva Masquerade blue tabby

Honed instincts

Domesticated relatively recently in animal history, cats retain some inklings of their conduct in the wild, which come across, for example, in their highly developed predatory behavior. A cat will immediately attempt to catch prey—namely most moving objects—without having been specifically trained to do so.

Cats possess certain instincts, or forms of hereditary inborn behavior, harking back to their past as free predators.

Some of the cat's physical characteristics are also directly inherited from life in the wild, beginning with its suppleness and ability to scale heights. Cats are naturally gifted climbers and have an innate litheness. They

---

Letting your kitten play

Play is essential to the kitten's harmonious behavioral development. Kittens initiate games from the age of three weeks, first with their siblings, then alone. The mother regulates her kittens' games, teaching them to control the intensity of their bites and to fix their own limits in their behavior. This is also when she teaches them about hygiene and grooming.

The cat should be able to continue to play in its new master's home and therefore needs toys to do so—as well as an owner who will look after and devote time to his feline friend!

also know instinctively how to use their claws to cling on and avoid a fall.

Predatory behavior is typical and, in the wild, is geared toward feeding. In a household, cats continue to exhibit this predatory behavior, but for their own enjoyment. It is developed naturally through the influence of play, learning by trial and error, or through imitation, by observing their mothers or other cats.

Enhancing the environment with toys, specific devices (cat trees), and scratching posts will allow the cat to work off surplus energy and to practice predatory behavior within the home, which is all the more essential if it cannot go outside.

Social skills

Socialization is a vital stage in a kitten's life. The foundations are laid during the first three weeks of existence and their repercussions will be felt throughout the cat's life.

There are two types of socialization: intraspecific (concerning its own feline species) and interspecific (concerning other species, including man).

Socialization with its own kind is the first to feature in the kitten's behavioral development and is essentially the responsibility of the mother. This is why it is so important to allow the kitten to grow up with its mother and siblings and not to be separated from them too soon. Once acquired, this type of socialization is irreversible and will last for life.

On the other hand, interspecific socialization, which occurs slightly later in the course of the development (yet in all cases should be introduced before the age of

To avoid any behavioral problems, kittens should not be separated too early from their mother and siblings

Like cat and dog! Cohabitation is easier if the animals are accustomed to it from a very young age

twelve weeks), is never acquired for good and requires regular "memory jabs." It is therefore the responsibility of the little feline's new master to take over from the breeder and to complete the process of interspecific socialization by handling the kitten and playing with it, introducing it to individuals of all ages and to other animals that it is likely to encounter later on (such as dogs or birds). Small cats should always be handled gently, in a non-traumatic manner.

It is important to familiarize the kitten with children, particularly if it has been raised in an adult environment. In return, children should also be taught to respect the cat and to avoid any unpleasant behavior toward it.

The rudiments of education

Teaching a cat requires time and patience. Cats will not learn by force, but only if they want to and enjoy doing so.

Education should begin upon the kitten's arrival and needs to be incorporated into play. It is also possible to use a cat's natural abilities, which are often self-taught (for example, opening a cupboard or putting their suppleness and agility to good use). These natural capacities can thus be turned to advantage. This method is known as "positive reinforcement." Play, rewards, and caresses are ways of showing a cat that it has done something good.

In all cases, education needs to be coherent. What is prohibited one day should not be permitted the next and vice versa—otherwise, the cat will become very confused.

Punishment: art and method

Cats are not punished in the same way as dogs. The basic rule is to prohibit the use of all direct corporal punishment, such as slapping or shouting. The cat would see this as a sign of aggression and act aggressively in return. The only possible negative technique should resort to external instruments such as water pistols or sprays of mineral water. They should be used skillfully as the cat must not associate with you the unpleasant sensation of the water spray. To be effective, the punishment should come "out of the blue" and take the cat by surprise.

Another possible method is to divert the cat's attention to something else. For example, if it starts to sharpen its claws on the couch, it can be diverted to the scratching post with the help of a tasty morsel or by throwing a ball and playing with it. Gradually it will come to understand that specific places are reserved for scratching.

Rewards, caresses, and compliments are all prescribed during the learning phase

When teaching things (e.g., walking on a leash, basic commands), importance should be given to caresses, games, and tasty rewards, although cats are more inclined to resist the call of food than dogs!

Calling by name should be used in a positive sense. It is, for example, inadvisable to call the cat by name if the cat is then to be punished. The main weakness of little felines is play, so priority should be given to exploring this area!

Some cats will even sulk when punished

at times serious aggressiveness toward man. In some cases, the cat will simply avoid contact with people, but in others it will attack them or become completely intolerant of contact.

Separating a kitten from its mother too soon may lead to other scenarios, notably that of hyperactive cats who have not learned to control their games and their bites or scratches and do not know when to stop a form of behavior.

The situation can almost always be put right by such measures as enhancing the environment, using pheromones on the advice of a veterinarian, the acquisition of a second cat to temper things, or providing outdoor access.

Gentleness and stability are two key factors in the readaptation of an anxious cat. A behavioral therapy, under veterinarian control, is very often necessary to put the cat back on track and reestablish harmony in the home.

The risks of insufficient education

Generally speaking, any error while the cat is very young—particularly concerning its socialization—may give rise to behavioral disorders. They may take the form of a whole range of symptoms, from simple fears to phobias, as well as aggressiveness.

Lack of socialization with their own kind may lead to aggressive behavior among cats living in the same household. The absence of interspecific socialization—with respect to humankind in particular—may generate

Consulting a behaviorist may be a conceivable option in the case of disorders such as anxiety
Facing page: American Curl kittens

Feeding your cat

The cat's food should provide all the nutriments it needs to live: proteins, glucides, lipids, minerals, and vitamins; in addition, water is essential to its survival.

With respect to proteins, cats are unable to synthesize a particular amino acid, taurine, which must therefore be supplied by their diet. Deficiencies in this amino acid may engender visual disorders, cardiac ailments, or reproductive problems. This specificity means that the cat is labeled a strict carnivore and it is imperative that animal proteins feature in its diet.

Generally speaking, the cat's dietary requirements are defined in relation to normal adult maintenance. They will vary for a female during gestation or lactation, kittens, older cats, or sterilized cats, who are more susceptible to weight gain.

Cats' taste buds are not very receptive to sweet flavors but can detect salty, sour, and bitter sensations very well.

Food preferences vary according to the individual and the diet they have been used to since infancy. Feline tastes are therefore not universal and not all cats go for fish—some prefer meat!

Cans, dry food, or homemade fare?

Some cat owners prefer to give their cat homemade food that they have prepared themselves. Due to the risk of this being unbalanced, certain rules must be respected—the presence of animal protein in sufficient quantities, vitamin and mineral supplements, nutritional balance, vegetable content, and monitoring of the size of portions.

More practical and naturally balanced, industrial foods are available in both dry and moist form. The majority of today's cat owners prefer dry cat food. As long as you choose quality products, this type of food combines nutritional balance, ease of use, and economy for the cat owner, as its cost is generally more

Facing page: cats like a tasty treat and can be pilferers!
Right: upmarket dry food makes it possible to meet all of the cat's nutritional needs

A bowl of cold water should always be on hand

attractive than that of domestic rations or moist food with a water content of almost 80 percent. Dry food is well suited to self-service, which is recommended for cats. However, you should be vigilant about water supply and be sure that some is always available. In addition to their ease of use, industrial foods are often what the cat prefers!

Adapting food

During gestation and lactation, females have specific dietary requirements, favorable to the kittens' healthy development and, later, to the production of quality milk. An underfed female will lose weight and will also produce less milk, thus affecting the kittens' growth. During lactation, the mother should therefore enjoy a

Above: a balanced diet contributes to the beauty of the coat
Following pages: obesity is a growing concern among cats so it is important to control the amount of food intake

diet that is richer in energy-giving foods, proteins, and minerals (specially formulated varieties are available in the stores and from veterinarians) and dished out in unlimited supplies.

Specific diets are not only restricted to females during gestation or lactation. Older cats should also be given a particular diet in order to compensate for the drop in appetite that often accompanies ageing, as well as to guard against certain ailments associated with old age (kidney problems in particular).

Veterinarians offer "health foods" that are specifically designed to be effective in the prevention of certain ailments (e.g., kidney stones, hairballs, tartar, etc.) or that sometimes form an integral part of the medical

prescription for sick cats such as specific foods for cats with renal insufficiency, diabetes, etc.

A kitten's special needs

Suckled by its mother until being weaned, the kitten is then introduced to solid foods, as the quantity of milk its mother produces is insufficient for covering its nutritional needs. This transition should be made progressively and introduced from the fourth or fifth week of life. It is completed around the seventh week.

After being weaned, kittens start on solids that are specifically formulated to cover the needs of their young age. Here again, industrial foods are available from veterinarians or in the stores.

If the kittens are orphaned or the mother produces insufficient quantities of milk, they may have to be bottle-fed with an alternative. This milk replacement or formula is available from veterinarians, who will advise as to its usage.

Preventing obesity

Obesity is a phenomenon on the increase in human society throughout the world. The problem also occurs in pets, and cats are no exception. In addition to its aesthetic consequences, obesity is dangerous on the grounds of the diseases it favors (including osteoarticular, respiratory, and cardiovascular disorders, as well as diabetes) and in the end entails a reduced life expectancy.

Fortunately this phenomenon is reversible and addressing the condition will improve the cat's health and quality of life.

To make a cat lose weight or simply to prevent the risks of obesity in an animal predisposed to this

Different foods exist for different ages and even breeds of cat

condition (including neutered and sedentary cats), dieting is not the only strategy. The effort should also extend to physical activity, an essential supplementary factor.

Dealing with overweight conditions entails a combination of dietary changes (e.g., reduced portions or "light" varieties of dry cat food), a change in dietary behavior (no longer dishing out tasty treats or giving in to a begging cat), and increased physical activity (toys and the use of devices such as cat trees to bring out its feline nature!).

If obesity is a long-standing problem in the cat, it is preferable to consult a veterinarian to draw up a diet program. The practitioner will help to construct a strategy to allow the animal to lose weight and provide medical monitoring of the excess pounds.

It is possible to combine business with pleasure by reconciling food with play. This may take the form of increasing the sources of food or of hiding them in various places around the home so that the cat must explore to find its sustenance. Another possibility is toys specifically designed to hold a few croquettes that are released when the cat mobilizes them.

Bones and milk: to give or not to give?
It is a mistaken belief that cats are born milk drinkers and that this foodstuff is all they need to be happy.

Self-service

Cats eat little but often (more than ten small meals a day). In this case, a self-service system suits them best. This system should, of course, be adapted to each particular case. For example, it would need to be reconsidered for a gluttonous cat that throws itself on its bowl and devours the contents as soon as it is filled.

A cat with a garden at its disposal will not resist the urge to hunt

Cow's milk should never be used as a substitute for water, the only drink that is really necessary.

As they grow older, some kittens lose their ability to digest the lactose in milk, as the enzyme required for this disappears with age. Therefore cow's milk is more often a source of diarrhea than pleasure!

Some cats are able to digest milk throughout their life, while others are not. For the latter, specific cat milk that contains no lactose can be found in stores, and some cats enjoy this.

It is likewise preferable to proscribe bones, which if ingested can generate risks for the whole digestive tract (risk of perforation of the esophagus or intestine), dangers of suffocation (a bone stuck in the throat), and risks of bleeding in the oral cavity. Being indigestible, bones also represent a frequent cause of constipation in the cat, which is a further reason to disallow them.

Left: overweight conditions or weight loss
require veterinary attention
Facing page: the joy of an after-dinner roll around

Feline health and grooming

For their own comfort, cats should be subjected to at least a minimum amount of attention regarding hygiene. Brushing gets rid of loose hairs and therefore prevents the formation of hairballs (trichobezoar) in the digestive tract, which are frequent causes of vomiting and digestive disorders (constipation). Brushing should therefore be done regularly and its frequency depends on the hair length and season—the annual spring and fall molt periods call for more sustained brushing. Occasionally, or before a cat show, brushing can be supplemented with a bath using a shampoo specifically formulated for cats. Some medicated shampoos are used in the medical treatment of certain skin disorders and are therefore available on veterinary prescription.

In addition to brushing, it is often necessary to clip the claws, particularly if the cat lives in an apartment, as the claws grow continuously. Care should be taken not to cut them too short so as to avoid touching the quick, the claw's pink base, which would bleed profusely.

Eye and ear care are the final items in this list of basic hygiene. Never use a cotton swab to clean a cat's ears. These little sticks might push the wax or dirt toward the eardrum rather than eliminating it. It is better to use an auricular solution specifically formulated for animals. The product is poured into the ear, and any

excess and the dirt that comes up to the surface are then wiped away using absorbent cotton or a handkerchief. Special ocular cleansers are available from the veterinarian and are useful for cats prone to eye watering, such as Persians.

No skipping parasite control

External (such as fleas and ticks) and internal (intestinal worms) parasites are unwanted guests, liable to become

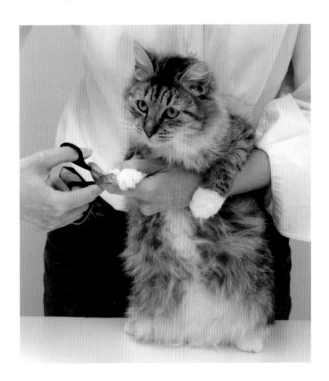

Preceding page: good regular brushing
prevents the formation of knots
Facing: when clipping the claws,
be careful not to touch the quick

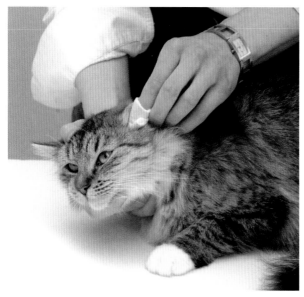

Regular ear cleaning helps to eliminates dirt
and to prevent certain ailments

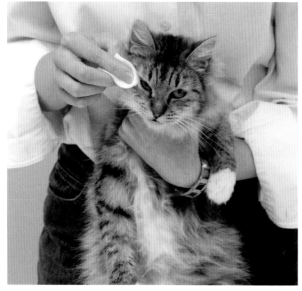

The use of specially adapted products
is recommended for cleaning the eyes

attached to your cat. Some measures are called for to prevent parasitism, which is the source of much discomfort.

To combat fleas and ticks, the rule is to apply external parasiticides. Many products available from veterinarians are considerably more effective with persistence over time. Used regularly and correctly, these products—which can take the form of sprays, collars, tablets, or pipettes to be emptied between the shoulder blades—are likely to provide your cat with effective protection against fleas (a source of itching), and ticks (carriers of what are sometimes serious diseases).

Besides these two common parasites, cats may fall victim to others that cause skin disorders such as ringworm or mange. Medical treatment is mandatory in such cases and requires veterinary consultation.

Regular worm treatment in line with a veterinary prescription is needed to prevent intestinal parasitism. In some cats, internal parasites may go by unnoticed, but they can also cause digestive disorders or slow development in kittens.

Worm treatment is all the more essential as many intestinal parasites found in cats are carriers of zoonoses (diseases that can be passed on from the animal to man and vice versa) and therefore liable to infect the owners. Feline worm treatments are highly effective nowadays and completely prevent such risks. The frequency of worm treatments varies according to the context and can be explained by the veterinarian.

Vaccinating to protect

Vaccination protocols may vary from one country to another. Thus, in the United States, manufacturers claim that certain vaccine strains and valences provide longer-lasting protection than those in other countries. Therefore annual vaccinations do not necessarily contain all valences, and some inoculations require

Regular vaccinations and worming throughout a cat's life will protect against many diseases and parasites

boosters only every two or three years according to laboratory indications. In North America, veterinary schools have highlighted the toxicity of certain vaccines for cats (and dogs), as well as the appearance of fibrosarcoma at the site of injection. This has led to a sense of disquiet among the heads of the veterinary pharmaceutical industry.

Veterinary products on sale in various countries do not necessarily bear the same name and are not necessarily identical. In the United States, for example, there exists a vaccine against feline infectious peritonitis (FIP), which is not marketed in France, despite this being a life-threatening disease.

Preventing domestic accidents

Veritable budding acrobats, kittens are always game for exploring something new, sometimes at their own risk! Houses do indeed conceal a certain number of dangers for our little feline friends and a few security measures are called for.

Access to balconies should be monitored as they involve the risk of falling. And unfortunately the theory that cats always fall on their feet does not always hold true.

Very playful, cats will not distinguish between a simple piece of string and an electric cable. Any wires trailing around should therefore be hidden as far as is feasible and, if possible, sockets protected.

Medicines and toxic substances should be placed out of cats' reach, in a secure place, as they represent potential sources of poisoning. Likewise, some houseplants (such as the ficus) are poisonous for cats. You should therefore check that a plant is not potentially toxic before allowing your cat to munch on the leaves!

Main diseases affecting cats

Cats are unfortunately not exempt from illness and are specifically associated with some infections.

Among the main feline ailments are infectious diseases such as feline leukemia virus (FeLV), feline infectious peritonitis (FIP), feline immunodeficiency virus (FIV), and typhus. Rapid tests, performed by the veterinarian, make it possible to detect cats infected with FeLV or FIV. These animals should then be kept away from healthy cats as they might pass on the disease to them. Not all cats infected with these viruses develop the disease. Some may remain healthy carriers and as such are even more of a danger to their own kind because they can transmit the virus insidiously. When the illness develops, FIV and FeLV generally lead to weakened immunity, which finds expression in the development of various infections.

There are two forms of feline infectious peritonitis (FIP): wet (effusive) and dry. Caused by a coronavirus,

Owners need to be vigilant to prevent
falls and domestic accidents

this disease is generally fatal. Typhus may have various consequences, but this virus can also lead to death.

Vaccination exists as the best means of prevention of some of these conditions (leukemia, typhus).

The term coryza is used to refer to infections of the upper respiratory tracts, but the etiologic agents responsible for such clinical signs (fever, eye watering, sneezing, nasal discharge) are variable and liable to act in combinations.

In addition to these viral diseases, bacterial infections can also afflict cats.

All the cat's organs—digestive tract, respiratory system, cardiovascular system, skin, eyes, and kidneys—can be affected by various ailments.

In 1996 a variant of Creutzfeldt-Jakob disease (vCJD) emerged. This strain is linked to a specific bovine ailment, bovine spongiform encephalopathy (BSE), still known as "mad cow disease." The infectious agent

Here, a healthy young female Bengal, brown spotted tabby

responsible is a prion, and diseases of this type have been found in other species, including cats. It is caused by eating infected beef. In England in 1990 a cat died of spongiform encephalopathy. While this remains an isolated case, it means that there is risk. Nowadays, cat food manufacturers carry out many tests and quality checks. There is therefore nothing to fear from industrial food, which is just as good as the human food industry.

Any change in your cat's behavior (such as refusal to eat, despondency, drinking more than usual, or feverish states) should prompt you to consult a veterinarian, as such symptoms, even if they appear insignificant, may conceal a much more serious disorder. The veterinary practitioner alone will be in a position to implement the necessary medical examinations to diagnose a possible ailment and to treat it.

Feline reproduction

Gestation lasts between sixty-three and sixty-six days in cats. Females give birth to an average of one to three kittens per litter, sometimes many more. A veterinarian can monitor the gestation, ensuring its smooth progress with the aid of X-rays and ultrasound scans. Female cats are distinctive in that several different males can inseminate them. The same father will therefore not necessarily sire all the kittens in the same litter.

Natural births are the norm and last from between one to eight hours, depending on the number of kittens. Human intervention is only required in the case of some particular incident; more often than not, it is enough to keep a discreet watch.

Cats generally make good mothers and give their kittens the care they need.

Is sterilization necessary?

Surgical sterilization, traditionally done around the age of seven months, is recommended for cats not intended

An initial visit to the veterinarian is a must when acquiring a cat. A European Shorthair kitten, black silver spotted tabby

Cats generally have natural births

There is soon a scramble to reach the teats!

for reproduction, due to the benefits it represents for both cat and owner.

For females, there are two possible spaying methods depending on the situation: the withdrawal of the ovaries (ovariectomy) or the removal of the ovaries and uterus (ovariohysterectomy). For males, the neutering operation consists of removing the testicles.

Besides removing the risk of unwanted gestations, sterilization has other advantages. If performed before the first heat in females, it significantly lowers the risk of the appearance of mammary tumors.

Neutering serves to reduce certain undesirable effects found in uncastrated males (such as running away to look for females in heat and the subsequent risk of traffic accidents, fighting between males, or urine marking). On the whole, these operations are beneficial to the cats' health and make for increased longevity.

Contraception using medications is possible, but in general, it is not recommended given the risk of harmful side effects.

A ticket to ride

The EU Pet Passport is a European regulation specific to travel between Member States. The *Pet Travel Scheme* (*Pets*) is a British initiative. It concerns cats but also covers dogs and ferrets. This scheme has made it possible to put an end to the quarantine regulations imposed on animals entering Britain from a trip abroad or arriving for the first time. Quarantine aimed to keep Britain a "rabies-free zone" and protected from other diseases, but it was very restrictive—very difficult "accommodation" conditions and high costs incurred for owners, who could not always be sure of getting their pet back alive at the end of this enforced period of custody.

Facing page: surgical spaying and neutering offer many advantages

It is quite possible to teach a cat to walk on a leash

Now by means of this passport, identified by an electronic chip (transponder)—the only recognized means of identification in Great Britain—and having undergone a whole array of mandatory tests (including a blood test to measure anti-rabies antibodies dating from less than three months ago), animals can breeze back and forth across the British border with their masters and return to the fold as if it were the easiest thing in the world. This marks a great change. The United States, Canada, and Norway are exempt from these obligations.

In all cases, whatever the country of destination, it is highly recommended that you consult the embassy of the country concerned in order to check the procedure to follow when traveling with a cat. Generally speaking, with the exception of Britain, it is advisable to be in possession of a valid health and vaccination certificate; the anti-rabies vaccination should date from more than one month but less than one year ago.

Feline ID

Cats can be identified by tattooing or, in recent years, by the subcutaneous implantation of a microchip also known as a transponder. A veterinarian intervenes in both procedures. Tattooing requires a general anesthetic. The transponder is implanted beneath the skin on the left side of the animal's neck. They may be used individually or in combination. It contains a code that can be read using a specific device found in the possession of veterinarians, customs officials, and some other structures (such as cat shows).

As of 2012, electronic identification will be the only ID procedure to be officially recognized and will therefore be essential if traveling abroad with your pet.

A carrying basket is ideal for traveling

When traveling within the European Union with a cat, not only must the owner be in possession of this passport, but he should also have attended to the cat's identification and anti-rabies vaccination. In addition, certain supplementary measures (rabies serology and specific parasiticide treatment) are required for travel to Britain, Sweden, Malta, or Ireland. All travel with cats to these nations therefore needs forethought, as the health conditions imposed require a lapse of time of a few months. Moreover, microchip identification is the only recognized form of ID in these countries.

Before any trip abroad with a cat—whether within Europe or another country—it is necessary to consult with a veterinarian and find out about the formalities required by the country of destination.

The makings of a champion

Cats have their own beauty contests! Key dates in a breeder's life, cat shows are a way of enabling him to assess his selection efforts. In these events, cats are judged according to breed, with their morphology being compared to that set down in their standard. The judge decides between the various individuals by awarding a score and, at the end of the competition, designates the best representatives of each breed, as well as the finest cat in the show.

Private individuals can show their cats or simply visit cat shows for the pleasure of looking. It is also an opportunity to discover the huge variety of feline species.

Shows are not only the prerogative of pedigree cats as, in most cat shows, there is a "house cat" category open to all cats, without pedigrees, on condition that they comply with the necessary health formalities.

Registration and handling procedures vary from one country to the next, as do the ways of exhibiting the cats and showing them to the judges. Breed clubs and cat federations in the United States all provide impressive information services compared to other countries. Not only do they explain what a pedigree cat is and how to select one, they also advise on how to show it for the first time. In the UK and the US for example, there are also categories reserved for household pets, contests for young handlers, and demonstrations of sporting activities for cats (an area hitherto the preserve of dogs). In the United States, unsterilized housecats can compete up to the age of eight months, after which they need to be spayed or neutered in order to continue to participate.

Beauty at a price

Getting your cat ready for a show requires time and patience. The extent of preparations vary, of course, according to the breed of cat and the density and length of its hair. A bath followed by careful drying and brushing are the basics for looking good. Conditioning treatments, talc, polishing with a chamois leather, or bran baths are also useful tricks.

Facing page: participating in cat shows provides a showcase for breeders' work on selections
A male American Curl Longhair, red tabby point
Right: making your cat into a beauty champion requires some sacrifices. A Somali, ruddy

Glossary

Some terms that occur in this book are specific to cat fancy and are used, particularly in the breed standards, to provide an accurate description of certain morphological characteristics.

Brown: A breed's genetically black color.

Cameo: A red, cream, or tortie coat with silver white base.

Cinnamon: A reddish-brown coat color.

Cobby: A compact, stocky, and broad, round body type, heavy boned and low on the legs.

Colorpoint: A coat pattern where the darkest color is restricted to the extremities of the body—the face mask, tail, feet, and ears—with much lighter shading on the body; blue eyes.

Fawn: Genetically corresponds to diluted cinnamon (see term above); a pinky beige buff color.

Foreign: The lightest of all medium conformation body types, a cat that is slim and elegant without going to extremes. Medium conformation body types are characterized by a rectangular body, a solid but fine bone structure, a wide but firm collar, medium tail, a modified wedge or wedge-shaped head, and round or oval paws.

Golden: A color comparable to that of a ripe apricot.

Lilac: A shade of pinkish beige.

Marble: Tabby (see term below) pattern, with ring-shaped designs (rosettes) on the flanks and perhaps the thorax.

Parti-colors: Cats of several hues.

Seal: Sometimes used to refer to black, particularly in Oriental breeds.

Silver: Coat ground color in some cats, usually the result of a white coat with black ticking (see below).

Smoke: Cat color that is white at the base and with darker coloring covering most of the hair shaft.

Sorrel: Color with a hint of chocolate, as in the Abyssinian for instance.

Spotted (spot): Small, distinctly colored markings distributed all over the body.

Tabby: Coat pattern that is either striped or mackerel, blotched or classic, spotted, ticked (see below), or "agouti" (each individual hair follicle having contrasting bands of color).

Ticked (ticking): Alternating bars of dark and light colors in the coat.

Tortie (tortoiseshell): A color mainly found in females, combining blue and cream, or black and orange.

Useful Addresses

US

The Cat Fanciers' Association, Inc.
1805 Atlantic Ave.
P.O. Box 1005
Manasquan, NJ 08736-0805
Tel.: (732) 528-9797 Fax: (732) 528-7391
www.cfainc.org

The American Association of Cat Enthusiasts, Inc.
P.O. Box 321
Ledyard, CT 06339
Tel.: (973) 658-5198
Fax: (866) 890-2223
www.aaceinc.org

The International Cat Association, Inc.
Animal House Shelter
P.O. Box 2684
Harlingen, TX 78551
Tel.: (956) 428-8046

Fax: (956) 428-8047
www.tica.org

American Society for the Prevention of Cruelty
to Animals (ASPCA)
424 E. 92nd St.
New York, NY 10128-6804
Tel.: (212) 876-7700
www.aspca.org

American Association of Feline Practitioners
203 Towne Centre Dr.
Hillsborough, NJ 08844-4693
Tel.: (800) 874-0498
Tel.: (908) 359-9351
Fax: (908) 359-7619
www.aafponline.org

CANADA

Canadian Cat Association / Association
Féline Canadienne
289 Rutherford Road, S #18
Brampton, ON L6W 3R9
Tel: (905) 459-1481
Fax: (905) 459-4023
www.cca-afc.com

Adoption Chats Sans Abri
557 Ch de la Canardière
Quebec, QC G1J 2B5
Tel.: (418) 522-7700
www.centreacsa.com

Ontario Society for the Prevention of Cruelty to Animals
16586 Woodbine Avenue, RR 3
Newmarket, ON L3Y 4W1
Tel.: (905) 898-7122 ext. 304
http://ontariospca.ca

AUSTRALIA & NEW ZEALAND
Australian Cat Federation Inc.
P.O. Box 331
Port Adelaide BC SA 5015
Tel.: (08) 8449 5880
www.acf.asn.au

The Governing Council of the Cat Fancy Australia and
Victoria Inc.
4/170 Underwood Road
Ferntree Gully, Victoria 3156
Tel.: (03) 9752 4217
www.cats.org.au

RSPCA Australia Inc.
P.O. Box 265
Deakin West ACT 2600
Tel.: (02) 6282 8311
www.rspca.org.au

Catz Incorporated
New Zealand National Registry For Cats
P.O.Box 100823
North Shore Mail Centre Auckland
www.catzinc.org.nz

New Zealand Cat Fancy Inc
Private Bag 6103
Napier
Tel.: (06) 839 7811
www.nzcatfancy.gen.nz

SPCA New Zealand
PO Box 15349
New Lynn
Auckland 0640
Tel.: (09) 827 6094
Fax: (09) 827 0784
http://rnzspca.org.nz

UK
Governing Council of the Cat Fancy
5 King's Castle Business Park
The Drove
Bridgwater
Somerset TA6 4AG
Tel.: 01278 427575
www.gccfcats.org

Cats Protection
National Cat Centre
Chelwood Gate
Haywards Heath
Sussex RH17 7TT
Tel.: (Switchboard) 08707 708 649
Tel.: (National Helpline) 08702 099 099
Tel.: (Adoption Centre) 08707 708 650
www.cats.org.uk

The Feline Advisory Bureau (FAB)
Taeselbury
High Street
Tisbury
Wiltshire SP3 6LD
Tel. outside UK: 01747 871 872
Fax: 01747 871 873
www.fabcats.org

INTERNATIONAL ORGANIZATIONS
SPCA International
The mission of SPCA International is to raise awareness of the abuse of animals to a global level, to teach and foster good pet parenting practices, and to promote spay and neuter programs around the world with the goal of eradicating the need to euthanize healthy and adoptable companion animals of all ages.
www.spca.com

World Animal Net
The world's largest network of animal protection societies with consultative status at the UN is working to improve the status and welfare of animals with over 3,000 affiliates in more than 100 countries.
www.worldanimal.net

Fédération Internationale Féline
A leading international cat fancier society.
www.fifeweb.org

World Cat Congress
Promoting harmony in cat fancy.
www.worldcatcongress.org

World Organisation for Animal Health
www.oie.int

Index

References

US Pet Ownership and Demographic Sourcebook, 2002
Pet Food Manufacturer's Association (PFMA)
International Conference on People and Animals: A
   Timeless Relationship, Glasgow, 2004
TICA (The International Cat Association)
Cat Fanciers Association (CFA)
Governing Council of the Cat Fancy

The International Cat Association (TICA)
American Cat Fanciers' Association (ACFA)
Cat Fanciers Federation (CFF)
Association féline canadienne (ACF)
Association of Pet Behaviour Counsellors
Voice for the Animals

Photographic credits

All photographs from Horizon Features (www.horizonfeatures.com) and Michel Viard, except:
29, 63 (K. Descamps); 37, 52, 75 (G. Félix); 24, 40–41, 43, 72, 85, 86, 90 (A. Guerrier); 17, 62 (L. Hégo); 55, 67, 80–81 (G. Ken); 23 (M. Luquet); 42 (B. Neveu); 69, 79 (P. Neveu); 2, 11, 14, 15, 26, 27, 30–31, 45, 50–51, 56, 60–61, 64, 66, 68, 70–71, 73, 74, 93 (N. Novack); 22, 92 (P. Raynaud); 7 (O. Soury); 8, 16, 19 (All rights reserved).

Translated from the French by Susan Schneider
Design: Nadège Deschildre/Studio Horizon
Copyediting: Karen Heil
Typesetting: Gravemaker+Scott, Edinburgh
Proofreading: Kate van den Boogert
Color Separation: Couleurs d'Image, Ivry-sur-Seine

Distributed in North America by Rizzoli International
Publications, Inc.

Originally published in French as *Chats*
© Flammarion S.A., Paris, 2007

English-language edition
© Flammarion S.A., Paris, 2008

08 09 10 3 2 1

ISBN-13: 9782080300669

Dépôt légal: 09/2008

Printed in Malaysia by Tien Wah Press